REMEMBER
TO BLOW SOAP BUBBLES
ONCE IN A WHILE.

THIS
BOOK OF HOPE
IS FOR ~~~~~~~~~~~~~~~~~~

Other Books By William Zimmerman

How To Tape Instant Oral Biographies

A Book Of Questions
To Keep Thoughts And Feelings

Make Beliefs

LIFE LINES

A BOOK OF HOPE

SOME THOUGHTS TO CLING TO WHEN
LIFE BRINGS YOU TOUGH TIMES

BY BILL ZIMMERMAN
DRAWINGS BY TOMBLOOM

GUARIONEX PRESS
LTD/NYC

LIBRARY OF CONGRESS CATALOGUE № 88.082746

ISBN 0.935966.04.8

THE AUTHOR WELCOMES YOUR COMMENTS AND SUGGESTIONS AS
WELL AS ANY LIFELINES THAT COME FROM YOUR EXPERIENCES.
PLEASE WRITE ··· WILLIAM ZIMMERMAN/GUARIONEX PRESS LTD
201 WEST 77 STREET
NEW YORK CITY 10024

THANK YOU.

>> SECOND PRINTING "1990" <<

DISTRIBUTED BY
THE TALMAN COMPANY

FOR

PAM, NICOLAS, SIMÓN·PEDRO AND MEGGIE,
THIS IS MY PANEL
FOR LARRY'S QUILT,
A MEMORIAL OF MY LOVE FOR MY BROTHER,

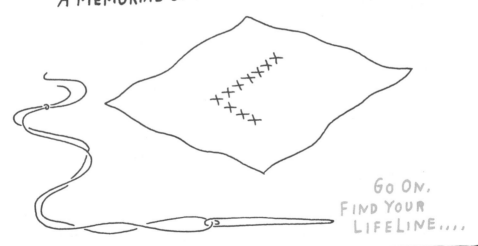

GO ON,
FIND YOUR
LIFELINE....

"Cálmate, corazón," my wife would coo to our little daughter when she cried so urgently in her arms. And sure enough, soon our child would feel comforted by the loving sounds, and stop crying. You see, *"Cálmate, corazón,"* means "Calm yourself, dear one" when translated from Spanish, and the words have magical soothing powers.

You will find the words used throughout "LifeLines." Simply put, this is a book of helping thoughts that offer comfort and hope to the child in each of us to get us through our lonely nights.

"LifeLines" provides a way to calm the desperate feelings we experience at times during our lives—fear, loneliness, great sadness and suffering.

You can ease these feelings by heeding some of the suggestions that appear after the words, *"Cálmate, corazón,"* on the following pages. Each thought has the power to provide an antidote to your pain and suffering.

I started writing these "life lines" during a plane trip to visit my brother who at the time was slowly dying. They gave me courage to overcome my fear of seeing him so and of ultimately losing him.

I completed these thoughts after he died as a way to come to terms with my grief and to create some meaning from the ashes of my pain. Perhaps, they will help you, too, in your own struggles.

You will find some "life lines" playful, some practical. All come from my heart as my way of trying to come to terms with the stresses and sorrows of daily living we share.

I hope you will find this book encourages you to search within yourself for your own "life lines" and to write your own thoughts on the blank pages provided in back should you wish. You can even color in the drawings if you like. When we come down to it, and we wake in the black night, we each have only ourselves to sit with through the dark. We need to find and coo kind, loving words to ourselves, the way my wife did for my little daughter.

Please accept "LifeLines," then, as a sign of recognition between you and me signifying that we experience many of the same feelings. These helping thoughts can be our lines to comfort.

Grasp them. You'll be safe.

P.S, FLIP THE PAGES,
AND WATCH THE DOLPHIN.

—BZ

LIFE LINE Nº 1

YOU WILL BE ALL RIGHT IF
YOU THINK OF
BEAUTY.

WHEN YOUR HEART
FEELS LIKE IT IS
BREAKING,

CÁLMATE, CORAZÓN,
(CALM YOURSELF, DEAR ONE,)

THINK OF BUTTERFLIES
LANDING ON YOUR WRIST,
OR BEAUTIFUL PHOSPHORESCENT
SPECKS
FLOATING DOWN AROUND YOU,

PUT WORDS ON PAPER
TO BAR THE UNHAPPINESS
THAT THREATENS TO
CHOKE YOU.

WHEN YOU
ARE SCARED
AND FRIGHTENED
AND YOUR HEART IS BEATING
SO QUICKLY,

CÁLMATE, CORAZÓN,
(CALM YOURSELF, DEAR ONE,)

TAKE PAPER AND PEN
IN HAND, AND WRITE ABOUT
WHAT'S FRIGHTENING YOU.

AFTER THE DARK EARLY MORNING
COMES THE SUNLIGHT
AND THE USUAL NOISE WE MAKE
EMBARKING ON OUR NEW DAY.

THE REGULAR PATTERN TAKES OVER,

WHEN YOU'VE GOT THE
MONDAY MORNING SHAKES "
THE WEEK
IS ABOUT TO BEGIN "
AND YOU ARE AFRAID,

CÁLMATE, CORAZÓN,
(CALM YOURSELF, DEAR ONE,)

START YOUR DAY BY LISTENING
TO A FAVORITE PIECE OF MUSIC; ITS
FAMILIARITY WILL EASE YOU ALONG.
TELL YOURSELF, " I AM STRONG, AND
WILL SURVIVE," THIS MONDAY MORNING,
TOO, WILL PASS, SOON IT WILL BE NOON.
SOON IT WILL BE TUESDAY. JUST KEEP
HOLDING ON.

WALK,
RUN,
TAKE ACTION,
DON'T JUST SIT THERE,
LET THE SUN SHINE UPON YOU,

WHEN YOU FEEL
YOUR WORLD HAS
COME TO AN END
AND YOU ASK WHY
BOTHER TO GO ON,

CÁLMATE, CORAZÓN.

FORCE YOURSELF TO JUMP UP
AND RUN FROM YOUR CARES.
LET THE COOL AIR TOUCH YOUR
FACE; SMELL THE GRASS;
FEEL THE SUN, AND SOON
YOU'LL REMEMBER HOW GLAD
YOU ARE TO BE ALIVE.

THE MORE
YOU GIVE TO OTHERS,
THE STRONGER YOU BECOME.

WHEN YOU FEEL
FRIGHTENED BY
SOMEONE'S DYING,

CÁLMATE, CORAZÓN.

GIVE THEM YOUR
LOVE AND CARE,
NOW.

LIFE LINE Nº 6

IT'S REALLY HARD TO GET
COMPLETELY LOST.

WHEN YOU'RE
AFRAID OF LOSING
CONTROL,

CÁLMATE, CORAZÓN,

LET YOURSELF GO
FOR A MOMENT,
EVEN TRY TO MAKE
A MISTAKE. THEN REGROUP.

GIVING TOO MUCH
AT ONCE
CAN BE OVERWHELMING.

LET YOUR LOVE
FLOW
EVENLY.

WHEN YOU WANT
TO GIVE THE WORLD
TO YOUR CHILD, WHO
REJECTS WHAT YOU OFFER,

CÁLMATE, CORAZÓN.

REMEMBER YOUR CHILD
CAN HANDLE ONLY A
SMALL PIECE AT A TIME.
SHE WILL RETURN WHEN
SHE HUNGERS FOR MORE.

LOVE
LIVES ON
IN MEMORY.

WHEN YOU
MISS A DEAD PARENT
SO MUCH THE PAIN
DIGS A PIT IN
YOUR STOMACH,

CÁLMATE, CORAZÓN.

SEARCH BACK
FOR A HAPPY MOMENT
YOU HAD TOGETHER,
AND REMEMBER,

THERE'S A TIME TO STOP
AND
TAKE STOCK,
SLOWLY.

WHEN YOU CAN'T
TAKE ANY MORE
PRESSURE,

CÁLMATE, CORAZÓN,

SHOUT TO THE WORLD,
"I'M GOING FISHING,"
EVEN IF YOU DON'T OWN
A ROD AND REEL.

THE OCEAN
ALWAYS
RENEWS US.

WHEN YOU ARE OUT
OF SORTS   AND
NOTHING FEELS
RIGHT,   THEM,

CÁLMATE, CORAZÓN,

TAKE A BREAK, GO TO THE
BEACH AND COLLECT SHELLS.
PLACE THEM ON A TOWEL IN
BEAUTIFUL PATTERNS TO DRY.
AFTERWARD, SMELL THE SEA.

FIND WHAT IS LIGHT AND FUNNY
IN YOU,
AND RECORD YOUR LAUGHTER
TO HEAR AGAIN AND
AGAIN
AND AGAIN AND
AGAIN.

IF YOU'RE AFRAID
YOU WON'T HAVE
ENOUGH MONEY FOR
YOUR OLD AGE,

CÁLMATE, CORAZÓN.

SIMPLY INSIST THAT
YOU'LL NEVER GROW UP
AND THAT YOU PLAN TO PUT
YOURSELF UP FOR ADOPTION TO
THE HIGHEST BIDDER. TO SWEETEN
THE POT SAY YOU'LL EVEN TOSS IN YOUR
WISDOM TO THE WINNER, THAT SHOULD
CLINCH IT,

YOU CAN NOT BE RESPONSIBLE
FOR EVERYONE AND EVERYTHING.
DON'T TAKE IT ALL
SO PERSONALLY,

NEXT TIME YOUR TEENAGE
DAUGHTER COMES HOME
SULLEN AND ANGRY AT
THE WORLD, INSTEAD OF
ASKING WHERE YOU WENT
WRONG AS A PARENT,

CÁLMATE, CORAZÓN.

GROWL AT HER. THROW IN A LOUD
BARK NOW AND THEN, BUT DON'T
FORGET LATER TO KISS THIS
ANGRY CHILD, SHE STILL NEEDS
TO BE LOVED.

KISS
THE SWEETNESS
WITHIN YOU,

WHEN YOU LOOK
TO GOD AND ASK,
"WHERE IS HE? I
CAN'T FIND HIM,"

CÁLMATE, CORAZÓN.

TAKE COMFORT IN THE STRENGTH
OF YOUR MIND AND SPIRIT TO
CREATE A REFUGE WITHIN
YOURSELF.

WE CAN HEAL OURSELVES
OVER AND OVER
AGAIN,

WHEN
YOU ARE RECOVERING
FROM A SICKNESS
AND FEAR YOU'LL NEVER
BE THE SAME AGAIN,

CÁLMATE, CORAZÓN.

REMEMBER,
THE CUT ALWAYS HEALS,
AND THE NEW SKIN
IS EVEN TOUGHER,

BE KIND
AND LOVING TO
YOURSELF.

WHEN YOU
HAVE TO DEAL
WITH SOMEONE
WHO INTIMIDATES
YOU,

CÁLMATE, CORAZÓN.

CONSIDER THAT THIS SAME
PERSON MUST DO THE
SAME FOOLISH THINGS YOU DO
EACH DAY. BRUSHING HIS TEETH OR
DRESSING TO HIDE HIS NAKEDNESS.
WE ARE ALL VULNERABLE,
AND, OH, SO HUMAN.

PUT AWAY THE
DEATH SONG,
PLAY THE FLIP SIDE,

WHEN SOMEONE
WHOM YOU LOVE
IS DYING BEFORE
YOUR EYES,

CÁLMATE, CORAZÓN.

PLACE YOUR LOVE INTO
LITTLE PACKAGES. MAKE THEM
A PRESENT OF YOUR LOVE AND
BLESSINGS, WRAPPED IN PRETTY
PAPER AND RIBBONS.

LOOK FOR THE FLOWERS,
THE BRIGHT COLORS IN YOU.
THEY ARE THERE,
WAITING
TO BE PICKED.

WHEN YOUR HOME
HAS BECOME A
BATTLEGROUND
WHERE HARD FEELINGS
AND ACCUSATIONS HAVE
BEEN AIRED,

CÁLMATE, CORAZÓN,

BRING HOME MANY BOUQUETS
OF FLOWERS AND STREW THEM
THROUGHOUT THE ROOMS, ON
THE FLOORS, IN THE BATHTUB, ON THE
BED, SMELL THE FLOWERS AS THEY
DEFEAT YOUR PAIN.

LIFELINE № 18

BEAT THE HARSHNESS AND PAIN
OUT OF YOUR HEART,

WHEN YOU CAN'T
HELP BUT THINK OF
ALL THE CARES AND
PROBLEMS THAT THREATEN
TO OVERTAKE YOU,

CÁLMATE, CORAZÓN,

MAKE BELIEVE EACH PROBLEM
IS AN EGG FROM YOUR
REFRIGERATOR. BREAK THEM
ONE BY ONE INTO A BOWL, AND
MAKE AN OMELETTE OF YOUR
TROUBLES.

When The Load
Is Too Heavy,
Bury The Cares
That
Weigh You Down.

IF YOU'RE CARRYING
THE WORRIES OF THE
WORLD ON YOUR BACK,

CÁLMATE, CORAZÓN.

DIG DEEP HOLES IN THE GROUND,
SAYING "GOOD RIDDANCE."
PLACE THOSE CARES,
ONE BY ONE, BENEATH
THE PILES OF DIRT.

Look To
The Familiar,
It Is Comforting,

WHEN YOU
FEEL YOU
CAN NO LONGER
HOLD ON,

CÁLMATE, CORAZÓN,

GET A BOTTLE OF YOUR
FAVORITE SODA, MAKE
SOME POP CORN, SWITCH
TO THE WORST "B" MOVIE
YOU CAN FIND ON TV,
AND INDULGE YOURSELF.

ALWAYS
REACH FOR THE STARS,
THEY ARE NOT
THAT FAR AWAY AND
THEY AWAIT YOUR
TOUCH.

WHEN
YOU FEEL
YOUR HEART
IS BREAKING,

CÁLMATE, CORAZÓN,

STICK YOUR HEAD OUT THE WINDOW,
LOOK UP TO THE STARS, IF YOU
CAN'T SEE THEM, THEN MAKE YOUR
OWN OUT OF TIN FOIL~CUT THEM
ANY SIZE YOU LIKE~AND PASTE
THEM TO YOUR CEILING, THINK OF
ALL THE POSSIBILITIES THERE ARE
BEFORE YOU,

MAKE SOMETHING
GOOD GROW
FROM THE BAD TIMES.

WHEN YOU ARE SAD,
AND THE TEARS KEEP
STREAMING DOWN
YOUR FACE,

CÁLMATE, CORAZÓN,

COLLECT THE TEARS
TO WATER YOUR PLANTS.

LifeLine No 23

SHARE
WHATEVER STRENGTH
YOU HAVE.
IT WILL HELP LIFT UP
THOSE WHO MAY
FEEL WEAK AND AFRAID.

WHEN YOU SEE
PEOPLE AROUND YOU
WHO ARE HURTING, AND
THEIR PAIN DISTURBS YOU,

CÁLMATE, CORAZÓN,

BE STRONG FOR OTHERS, USE
YOUR ENERGY TO COME OUT
OF YOURSELF, TO GIVE SOMETHING
TO THOSE IN NEED, BE IT A FLOWER,
OR SOME SPECIAL FOOD YOU HAVE
PREPARED, OR JUST A KNOWING SMILE,

SEEK THE SOFTNESS
INSIDE YOURSELF.

WHEN
YOU FEEL
LIKE GIVING
UP,

CÁLMATE, CORAZÓN,

TAKE THE CLOUDS
IN YOUR HAND
AND MUFFLE
YOUR DESPAIR
WITH THEM,

LIFE LINE №25

THERE ARE
SMILES AND LIGHT
WITHIN YOU,
REACH DEEP AND
LET THEM OUT,

WHEN THE TEARS
WON'T STOP WHILE
YOU'RE WALKING
ALONG THE STREET,

CÁLMATE, CORAZÓN.

LOOK FOR YOUR REFLECTION
IN A WINDOW. SMILE,
CATCH THE SUNLIGHT IN
YOUR HANDS AND WASH
YOUR FACE WITH IT.

TRANSFORM WHAT IS BAD
INTO SOMETHING GOOD.
YOU CAN DO THIS
IF YOU ARE
WILLFUL.

WHEN YOU HAVE
SO MUCH HATE
IN YOUR HEART
THAT IT'S LIKELY
TO DESTROY YOU,

CÁLMATE, CORAZÓN.

READ THE SUNDAY COMICS
OR BUY A JOKE BOOK.
THEY WERE CREATED
TO BRING A SMILE
TO YOUR FACE,

Look
To Your
Love
Of Beauty.

WHEN A
SAD MEMORY
BEGINS TO
SPOIL YOUR DAY,

CÁLMATE, CORAZÓN,

TAKE THE PETALS
FROM A FLOWER AND
PLACE THEM IN A SMALL
BOX THAT YOU CAN CARRY
WITH YOU AND SMELL
FROM TIME TO TIME.

You Needn't
Always
Confront a Problem
Head On,
Giving Yourself
Time Alone
Can Often Be The Kindest
Thing To Do,

WHEN YOU
HAVE TROUBLE
DECIDING WHAT
TO DO NEXT
WITH YOUR LIFE,

CÁLMATE, CORAZÓN.

TAKE THE FOG
TO WORK WITH YOU
IN YOUR BRIEFCASE,
IT WILL HIDE YOUR
INDECISIONS.

PERSIST
WITH ALL YOUR
STRENGTH
WHILE THERE IS AN
OUNCE
OF LIFE WITHIN YOU.

WHEN SOMEONE
ASKS YOU FOR
SOMETHING,
BUT YOU FEEL AS IF
YOU HAVE NOTHING
LEFT TO GIVE,

CÁLMATE, CORAZÓN.

BREATHE IN THE AIR
TO MAKE YOU STRONG
AND POUND A RHYTHM
WITH YOUR HANDS TO
INVOKE THE SPIRITS OF
STRENGTH AND SUSTENANCE,

Remind Yourself
Of What Has Given You
Warmth And Comfort,
There Are Times
When You Must Honor The
Past,

IF YOU FEEL
LIKE RUNNING
AWAY,

CÁLMATE, CORAZÓN.

GO TO THE KITCHEN
AND SMELL ALL THE
HERBS AND SPICES THAT
MAKE YOU FEEL SAFE,
SECURE AND AT HOME.

Invent
The Life
You
Want To Live.

WHEN YOU FEEL
SO TIRED AND
CANNOT CATCH
YOUR BREATH,

CÁLMATE, CORAZÓN.

MAKE BELIEVE THAT
THE WORD "TIRED" HAS NEVER
BEEN DEFINED. THINK OF
YOUR EXISTENCE WITHOUT
HAVING TO ENDURE THAT WORD.

FIND WAYS
TO LET
YOUR SPIRIT SOAR
AND LET YOUR
CARES FLY AWAY.

WHEN YOU DON'T KNOW
WHAT TO DO WITH ALL
THE PROBLEMS YOU HAVE,

CÁLMATE, CORAZÓN.

TAKE A BUNCH OF BRIGHTLY
COLORED BALLOONS, MARKING
EACH ONE WITH A PROBLEM,
LET THEM FLOAT INTO THE SKY.

Your Imagination
Is Stronger
Than Your Fears
Will Ever Be.

WHEN YOU ARE
DISTRESSED BY
THE PEOPLE WHO
FRIGHTEN YOU,

CÁLMATE, CORAZÓN.

SET UP A ROW OF CANDLES
TO REPRESENT THOSE WHO
ARE GIVING YOU A HARD TIME.
LIGHT THE CANDLES AND
WATCH THEM MELT DOWN UNTIL
THEIR FLAMES ARE
EXTINGUISHED.

WITH HOPE
IN YOUR HEART,
THE DEATH SPIRIT
CAN BE
OVERCOME.

IF
YOU ARE
VERY
FRIGHTENED
BY DEATH,

CÁLMATE, CORAZÓN.

TURN TOWARD THE MOON
AND GAZE AT ITS BEAUTY,
THE MYSTERY WILL
ENTHRALL YOU.

Your Inner Strength
Can Subdue Your Demons,

WHEN THERE IS
HATE IN YOUR
HEART,

CÁLMATE, CORAZÓN.

PUT YOUR RAGE AND ANGER
IN A SMALL CARTON THAT
YOU CAN KICK AROUND THE
ROOM. THEN SIT ON IT,
SQUASHING IT, SO IT WILL
NEVER HURT YOU AGAIN.

LET YOUR SENSES TAKE
YOU OVER.

FEED YOUR HUNGER FOR
LIFE,

IF
AT EVERY
TURN YOU FIND
THAT YOU ARE
TREMBLING,

CÁLMATE, CORAZÓN.

GO TO A FIELD TO PICK
A BASKET OF STRAWBERRIES.
DO YOU REMEMBER HOW GOOD
THEY TASTE WHEN THEY'RE
FRESH?

RECALL
ALL THE GOOD TIMES,
THEY ARE
SO MUCH BETTER
THAN THE BAD ONES,

NEXT TIME
YOU FEEL
LIKE NOTHING
GOES YOUR WAY,

CÁLMATE, CORAZÓN,

THINK OF THE MAGICAL
TIMES WHEN AS A CHILD
YOU WENT WITH YOUR
MOTHER OR FATHER TO A
FAVORITE STORE THAT HAD ALL
THE THINGS YOU WANTED MOST.

You Can Dream
Yourself Away
From All
Of Your
Hurts.

WHEN YOU
BECOME
FRANTIC AND
DESPERATE,

CÁLMATE, CORAZÓN,

IMAGINE HOLDING
THE STARS AND
THE MOON
IN YOUR
HANDS,

RECALL THE SEA,
HOW IT SMELLS AND SOUNDS.
THE SEA
WILL SOOTHE YOU.

WHEN YOU ARE ABOUT
TO START A NEW JOB
OR GO TO A NEW SCHOOL,
AND YOU ARE FILLED
WITH WORRY,

CÁLMATE, CORAZÓN.

PLACE A SHELL
TO YOUR EAR
AND LISTEN
TO ITS SONG.

LIFELINE No 40

GIVE YOURSELF SOME
TIME TO HEAL,
YOUR HURTS WILL GROW
WEAKER AND WEAKER
AS YOUR LIFE
TAKES OVER.

WHEN SOMEONE YOU
LOVE
HAS LEFT YOU,

CÁLMATE, CORAZÓN.

FIND A DRUM
AND BEAT THE
PAIN OUT OF
YOUR HEART.

DON'T FORGET
TO COUNT YOUR VICTORIES
ONE BY ONE,
LOVE THE GOODNESS
OF THE LITTLE CHILD IN YOU
AND BE MORE GENTLE
WITH YOURSELF,

WHEN YOU HAVE
DONE YOUR BEST,
BUT FAILED, AND
FEEL DIMINISHED,

CÁLMATE, CORAZÓN,

MAKE BELIEVE YOU ARE ADOPTING
YOURSELF AS A CHILD, THEN WITH
THAT CHILD IN HAND, SAY AT LEAST
THREE GOOD THINGS ABOUT YOURSELF,
MAKE A LIST OF YOUR STRENGTHS, OF
WHAT YOU HAVE BEEN ABLE TO
ACHIEVE, PLACE THIS IN A
SPECIAL SPOT THAT YOU CAN
COME BACK TO, ADD TO THE
LIST, SEE IT GROW.

Hang On
To Your Dreams,
In Them Resides Your Will
To Live.

WHEN YOU HAVE
SUFFERED A LOSS,

CÁLMATE, CORAZÓN,

THINK OF THE TINY ANT
WHO KEEPS REBUILDING,
CARRYING WEIGHTS MANY
TIMES ITS SIZE. IF IT CAN
DO IT, SO CAN YOU.

YOU CAN
NEVER REALLY RUN OUT
OF VISIONS OF HOPE,

WHEN YOU FEEL
YOU ARE BREAKING
INTO LITTLE PIECES,

CÁLMATE, CORAZÓN,

GO TO THE LIBRARY OR
YOUR FAVORITE BOOKSTORE,
TAKE COMFORT IN ALL
THE WONDERFUL BOOKS
THERE ARE YET TO
READ, WHOLE NEW
WORLDS TO EXPLORE
IN YOUR LIFE AHEAD,

You Are Much Stronger
Than You Realize.
Know That Jitters
Belong Only
In A Jitter Bag, Not
Within Yourself.

WHEN
YOU HAVE
A CASE OF
THE JITTERS,

CÁLMATE, CORAZÓN.

PLACE THEM
IN A PAPER BAG
THAT YOU CAN BLOW UP
AND BURST. AFTER YOUR
JITTERS FLY OUT, SING
"I'M ALIVE. I'M ALIVE.
I AM NOT DEAD. I WILL
SURVIVE."

NEVER LOSE SIGHT
OF WHAT IS
SPECIAL ABOUT YOU,

IF YOU LOSE
YOUR SELF·ESTEEM,
AND SEEM TO BE
SHRINKING,

CÁLMATE, CORAZÓN.

WRITE AN ANECDOTE
ABOUT YOURSELF,
CAPTURING THE BRAVEST DEED
YOU HAVE EVER DONE. SEARCH
IN YOUR MEMORY FOR THAT
SPECIAL SOMETHING.
IT WILL BE THERE,

WE CAN BECOME
A BETTER PERSON
WHEN WE GIVE OURSELF
THE SECOND CHANCE
WE WOULD GIVE TO OTHERS.

When Someone
You Have Counted
On Lets You Down,

Cálmate, Corazón,

Remember The Times
In Your Life When
You Did Not Come Through
For Someone But Were
Given Another Chance
To Make Good.

BE STUBBORN
AND STAND UP
FOR YOURSELF.

WHEN EVERYONE
SAYS "NO"
BUT THE ANSWER
YOU SEEK IS "YES",

CÁLMATE, CORAZÓN.

NEVER ACCEPT "NO"
FOR AN ANSWER. "NO" IS
JUST THE CLOSING OF A
DOOR WHICH YOU CAN OPEN
IF YOU TRY.

TOUCH SOMEONE
WARM AND LOVING.

WHEN
YOU FEEL
ALL ALONE,

CÁLMATE, CORAZÓN.

HUG YOUR DOG,
LOVE HER A LOT,

THINK
OF THESE GOOD THINGS
TO DO,
THAT CANNOT FAIL
IN HELPING YOU,

WHEN LIFE
IS JUST PLAIN
HORRID, AND A
WRINKLE'S ON
YOUR FOREHEAD,

CÁLMATE, CORAZÓN.

SKIP DOWN SOME EMPTY ROAD
THE WAY YOU DID AS A KID.

FIND A SWING AND START
PUMPING.

TAKE SOME COLORED CHALK
AND SKETCH ON THE SIDEWALK.

Start a Fresh Box Of Crayons
With a New Coloring Book.

Catch Some Sunshine In a Room
And Enter When You're Filled
With Gloom.

Keep a Magic Treasure Chest
Filled With Feathers And Stones
And Ribbons And Poems.

LIFE LINES
ONE LINERS

CATCH THE RAINFALL FROM THE SKY
AND DRINK IT WHEN YOU'RE FEELING DRY,

COLLECT SOME FALLEN AUTUMN LEAVES,
WRAP THEM WITH RIBBON FOR WHEN
YOU GRIEVE,

IN THE MORNING GO TO THE PARK AND
PICK UP PINE CONES UNTIL IT'S DARK,

WATCH A GROOVY
CHEECH & CHONG MOVIE,

LIFE LINES

CLOSING LINES

LET YOUR IMAGINATION
BE UNFURLED,
SO THAT YOU MAY WILL
A BETTER WORLD.

LIFE LINES

SUMMATION

YOU CAN HOLD ON WITH LOVE, ANGER,
FRIENDSHIP, GOOD WILL, STUBBORNNESS, FEAR,
WILL POWER, TERROR, CURIOSITY, AND
OLD·FASHIONED SPUNK.

You Can Heal Yourself Through Humor, Laughter, Fun, Absurdity, Silliness, Tears, Idiocy, Lunacy, Giggles, Good Feeling, Generosity, And Mostly Through Your Imagination.

Try, Try Your Best.

 And Don't Forget How To Smile.

LifeLines

To Call Your Own

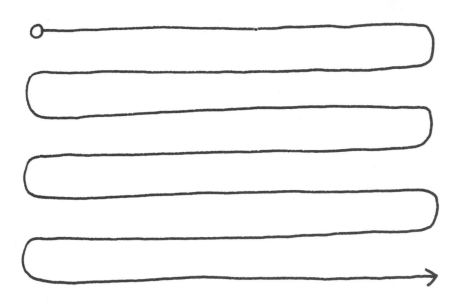

LifeLines
For a Lifetime

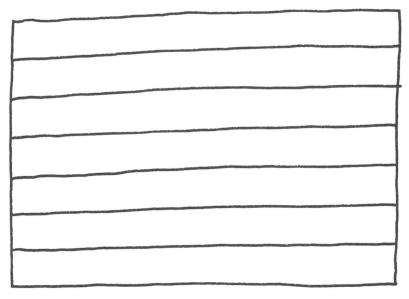

LIFE LINES
FINE LINES

LIFE LINES
END OF THE LINE

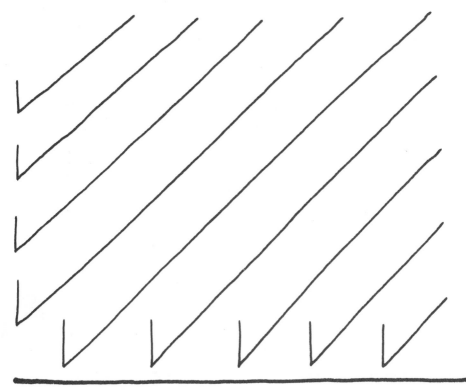

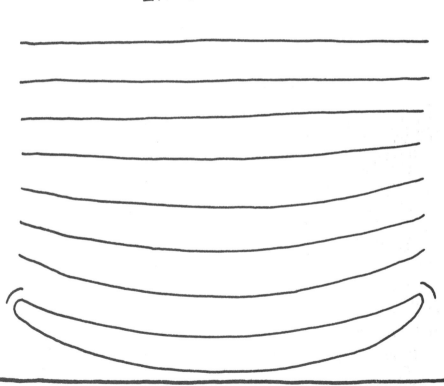

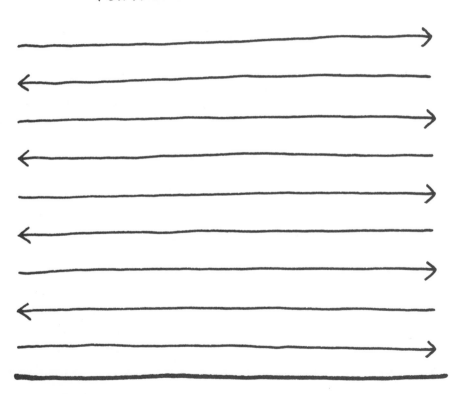

LIFE LINES

FOR A SENSE OF DIRECTION

LifeLines
Express Lines

LIFE LINES
BETWEEN THE LINES

)   (

)   (

)   (

)   (

)   (

)   (

)   (

)   (

LIFE LINES
FOR YOUR VERY OWN

LifeLines
For a New Beginning

Bill Zimmerman, the creator of "LifeLines," has been a questioner all his life. A journalist for more than twenty years, Mr. Zimmerman's first book was "How to Tape *Instant* Oral Biographies," a book that shows people how to interview relatives and friends and to capture on tape —audio and video—their life stories, memories and traditions. His second book, "A BOOK OF QUESTIONS to keep thoughts and feelings," is a new form of diary/journal with a special question-answer format that encourages people to write down what they think and feel. His third book was "MAKE BELIEFS," a gift book for the imagination that readers can complete with pencil, crayon or paintbrush. It has also been translated into Japanese and is a bestseller in that country.

Zimmerman's "life line" is: *Have hope in your heart.*

Tom Bloom divides his time between dreaming and drawing for The New York Times, The New Yorker, Atlantic Monthly, Fortune and others. He spends most of his time on this planet in New York City where he lives with a wife and a child.

Bloom's "life line" is: *Set out to capture your thoughts and dreams and you will have a most rewarding journey.*

P.S. NOW FLIP BACK THE PAGES, AND WATCH THE DOLPHIN PLAY,

Gifts for People You Care About
From Guarionex Press

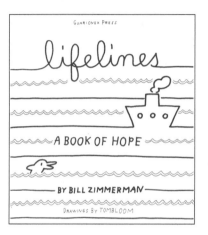

**GUARIONEX
PRESS, LTD.**

*Books that affirm the power
of the imagination and human spirit
to overcome life's problems.*

GUARIONEX PRESS (pronounced Gwah-ree-oh-nex) was named after a proud Taino Indian chief who lived in Puerto Rico in the sixteenth century. He fought bravely and fiercely against the Spanish, leading the last major Indian insurrection against the war-hardened, better-armed Spanish Army. When my wife, Teodorina, (who is Puerto Rican), and I decided to start our kitchen-table press in 1979, we knew we, too, would have to be brave and fierce in order to survive as a small business in a very competitive world. Se we named our dream press, Guarionex.

---BZ